រឿងនិទានៃនលេខ

THE NUMBER STORY

SMALL BOOK ONE

ENGLISH - KHMER

Numbers Teach Children
Their Number Names

written and illustrated by

MISS ANNA

Early Reader Edition of *The Number Story 1*
Bronze Medal Winner, 2016 Wishing Shelf Book Award

Cover by Jieeun Woo| Lumpy Publishing
Layout by Jieeun Woo| Lumpy Publishing
Translated by Soriyavithya
Coloring by Jieeun Woo and Maria Mirabella

Library of Congress Control Number: 2018902040

Names: Miss Anna, author.
Title: Number story : numbers teach children their number names / Miss Anna.
Description: Portland, OR: Lumpy Publishing, 2018.
Identifiers: ISBN 978-1-945977-82-4| LCCN 2018902040
Summary: The pictures and rhymes present stories which introduce numbers 0-10.
Subjects: LCSH Numeration—English--Khmer--Pictorial works--Juvenile literature. | BISAC JUVENILE NONFICTION /
Languages: English--Khmer
Classification: LCC QA141.3 .M57 2018 | DDC 513—dc23

Publisher: Lumpy Publishing
Website: www.missannabooks.com
Email: missanna@missannabooks.com
Facebook: Miss Anna Lumpy

Paperback: ISBN 978-1-945977-82-4
Printed in the U.S.A.   1 3 5 7 9 10 8 6 4 2

ចង់ រៀនអំពីឈ្មោះនៃលេខ?

It is very easy and a lot of fun!

រាជាការងាយស្រួល និងថែមទាំងសប្បាយខ្លាំង!

Say-along our little jingle

និយាយតាម ចំរៀងខ្លីរបស់យើង!

starting from Number One!

គោះយើងចាប់ផ្ដើមពីលេខមួយ!

1

ONE   looks like my one finger.

១ ☆ មួយ

វាមើលទៅដូចជាម្រាមដៃរបស់ខ្ញុំ។

ONE!
 មួយ!

2
TWO   trails a tail.
២ ពីរ
រ៉ាមានកន្ទុយៗ

A TAIL!
កន្ទុយ!

3

THREE   has bumps.

៣ ⋆ បី

រ៉ាម៉ានរបស់រលោក់ៗ

មើលរបស់រលាក់ទាំងអស់នោះ!

4

FOUR   carries a sail.

៤ ⋆ បួន

រាគឺជាទូកក្តោង។

A SAIL!
ក្តោង!

5
FIVE   is a racing track.
៥ ប្រាំ
គឺជាជានប្រណាំងៗ

VROOM
1

6

☆ SIX   curves like a snail.

៦ ☆ ប្រាំមួយ
រាកោងដូចខ្យង។

A SNAIL!

7

SEVEN has a sharp angle.

៧ ⋆ ប្រាំពីរ
រ៉ាមានមុំមុតស្រួច។

OUCH!
ឱ៊ិយ!
BE CAREFUL! IT'S SHARP!
ប្រយ័ត្នប្រយែង! វាគឺមុតស្រួចៗ

8

EIGHT   is rollercoaster rails.

៨ ∗ ប្រាំបី

គឺជាផ្លូវដែកសម្រាប់រថភ្លើងលេឿនលឿន។

เย้!
YIPPEE!

NINE   is a bubble on a stick.

៩ ប្រាំបួន

វាគឺជាពពុះនៅលើឈើៗ

A BUBBLE!
ពពុះ!

TEN   is an eye of a whale.

១០ ☆ ដប់

រាគឺជាភ្នែកម្មាងនៃត្រីបាឡែនៗ

មិចភ្នែក!
WINK!
HELLO! សួស្តី!

And និង 0
ZERO   is an empty pail.
0 ★ សូន្យ
វាគឺជាធុងទឹកទទេ។

IT'S
EMPTY!
វាគឺទទេៗ!

Thank you for playing with us today.

We had a lot of fun too!

អរគុណដែលបានលេងជាមួយយើងនៅថ្ងៃនេះ។

យើងក៏មានការសប្បាយខ្លាំងណាស់ដែរ!

We are your Number friends,
Zero to Ten,
Who will be here for you~

យើងគឺជាមិត្តភក្តិរបស់អ្នក។
សូន្យទៅដប់។
យើងនឹងនៅទីនេះសម្រាប់អ្នក។

Bye-bye now!
See you again soon!

លាហើយឥឡូវនេះ!
ជួបគ្នាម្ដងទៀតក្នុងពេលឆាប់ៗនេះ!

The Numbers are *SINGING* too!

To sing-a-long, look for Miss Anna Number Story
at your favorite music store like iTUNES.

MP3

Numbers 0-10
IDENTIFYING
& COUNTING

Numbers 11-20
& Ordinals

first, second, third...

Numbers 0-100
& Place Values

ones, tens, hundreds...

About Clocks
& Telling Time

hours, minutes, seconds

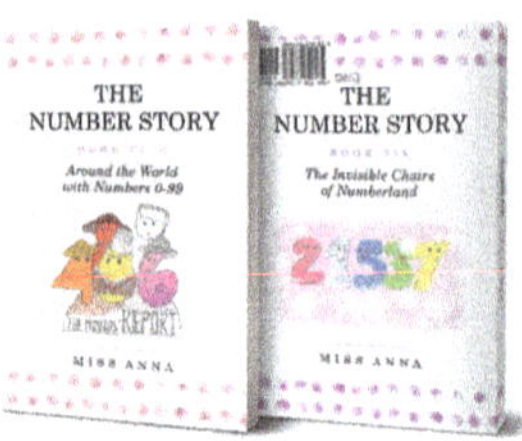

Number Story 1 & 2

isbn: 978-0-996216-48-7

Number Story 3 & 4

isbn: 978-1-945977-01-5

Number Story 5 & 6

isbn: 978-1-945977-06-0

Number Story 7 & 8

isbn: 978-1-949320-40-4

For more Miss Anna books to love,
visit us at

w w w . m i s s a n n a b o o k s . c o m

Numbers are working hard all over the world!
Come Travel the World with Us!

www.ingramcontent.com/pod-product-compliance
Lightning Source LLC
Chambersburg PA
CBHW040902070726
47599CB00035B/2274